# THIS BOOK BELONGS TO

........................................

# COLOR TEST

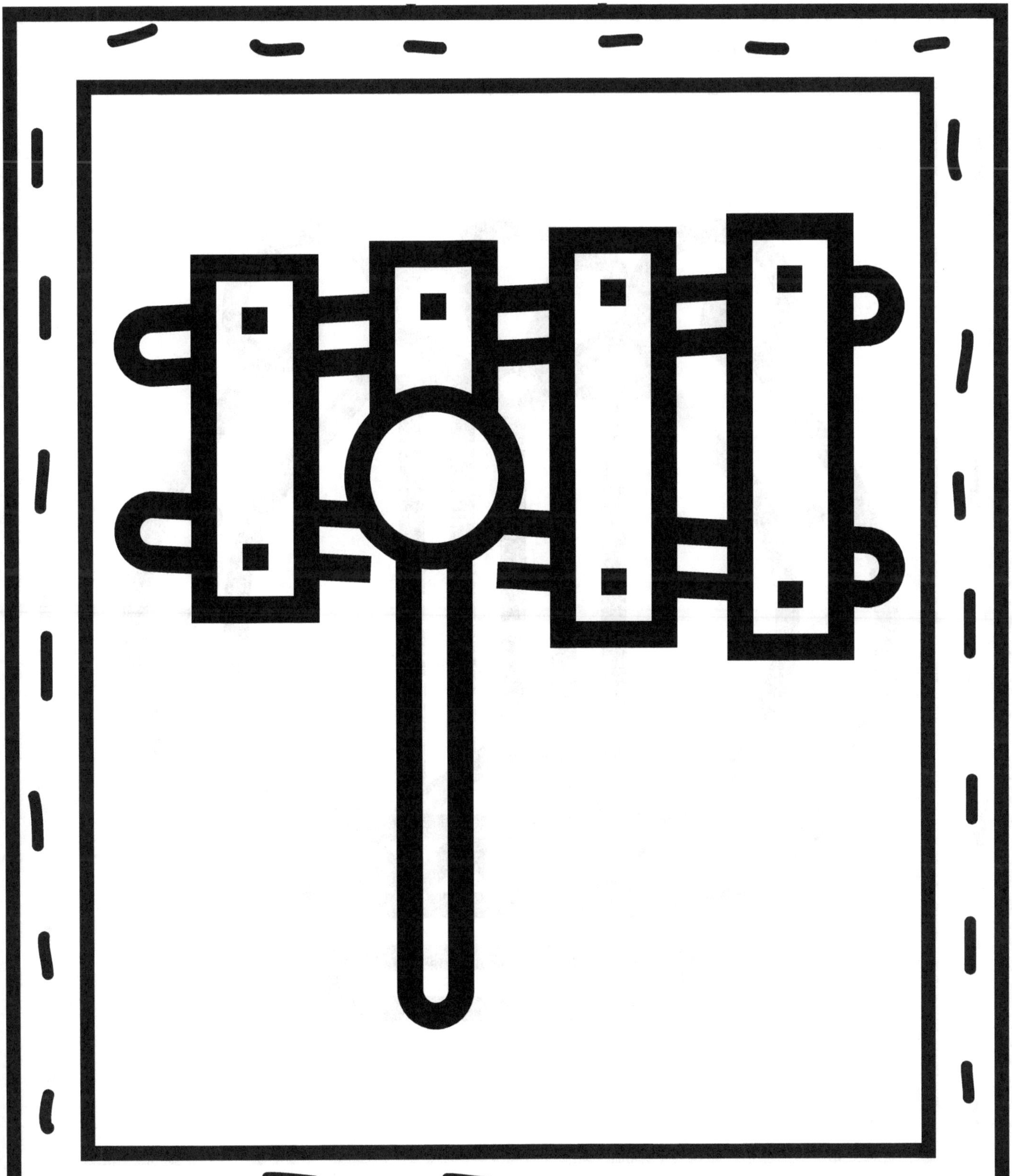

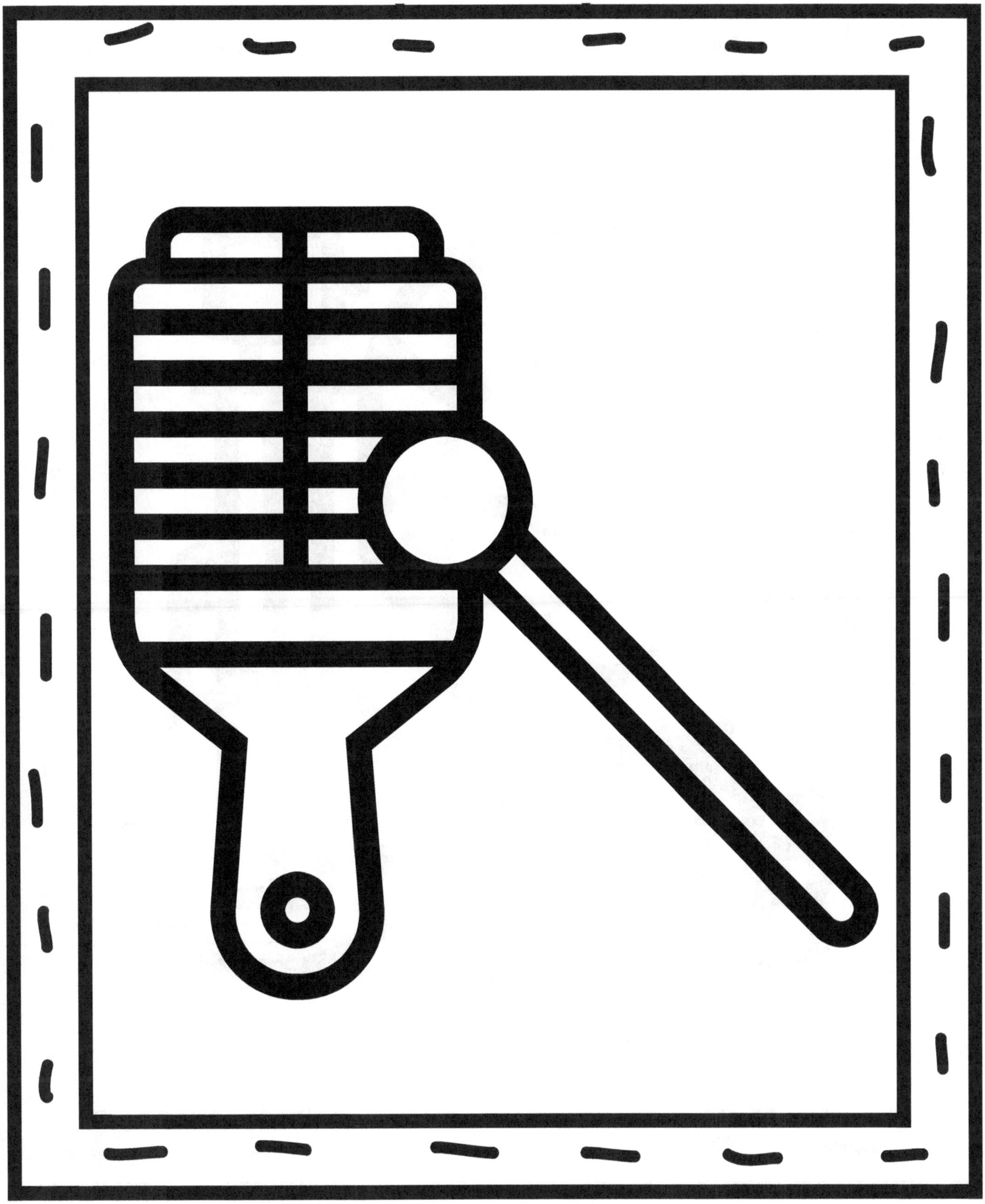

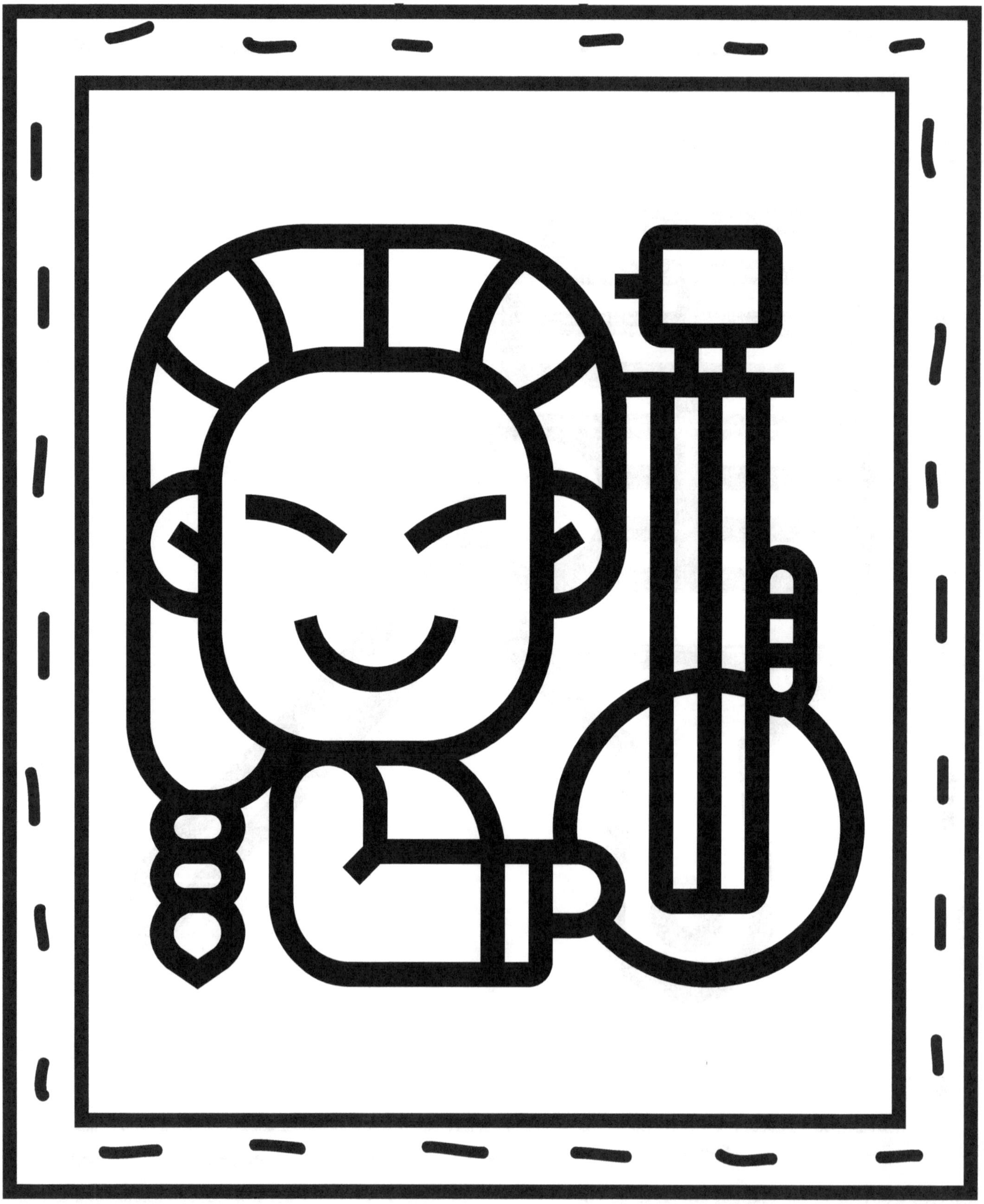

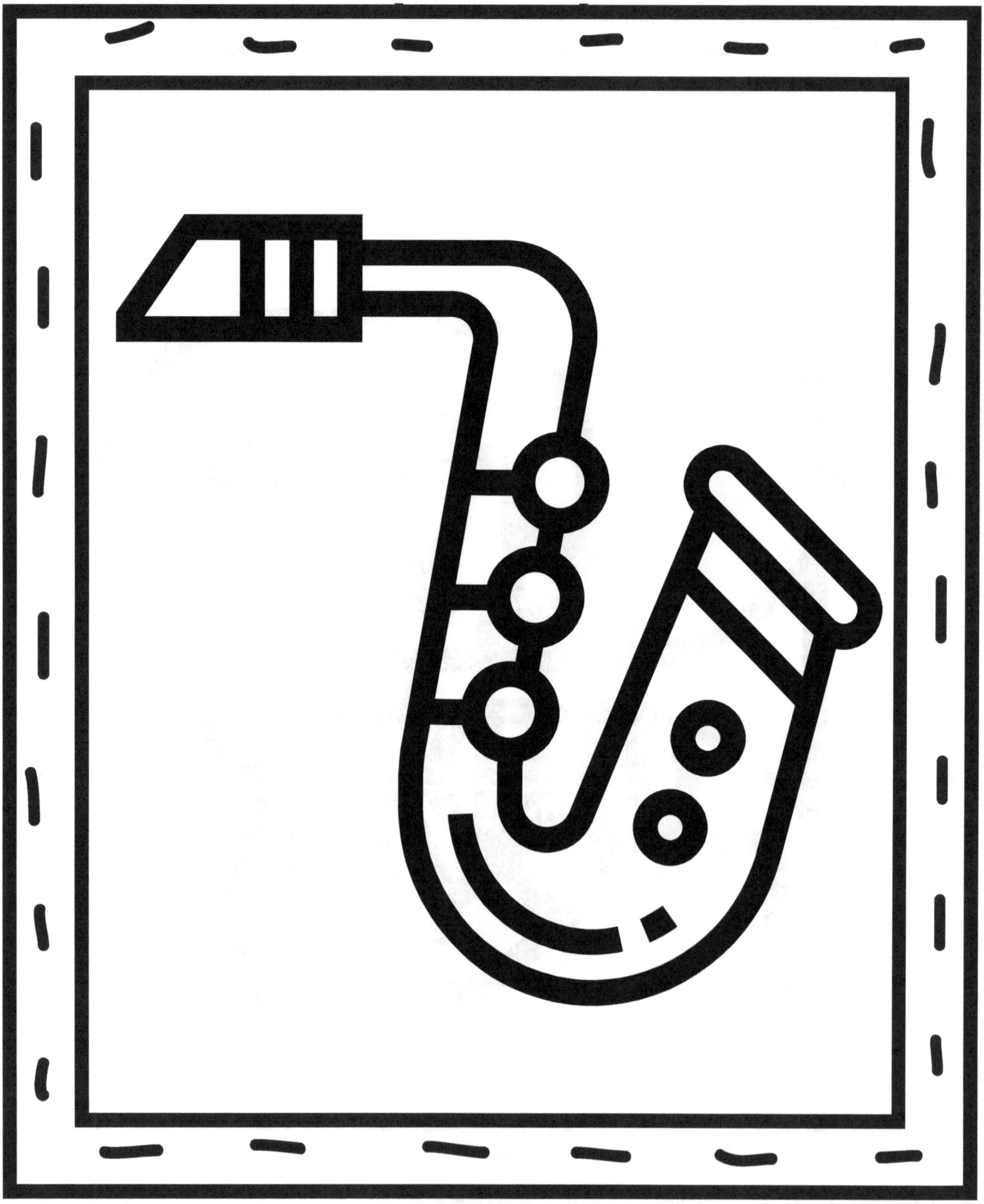

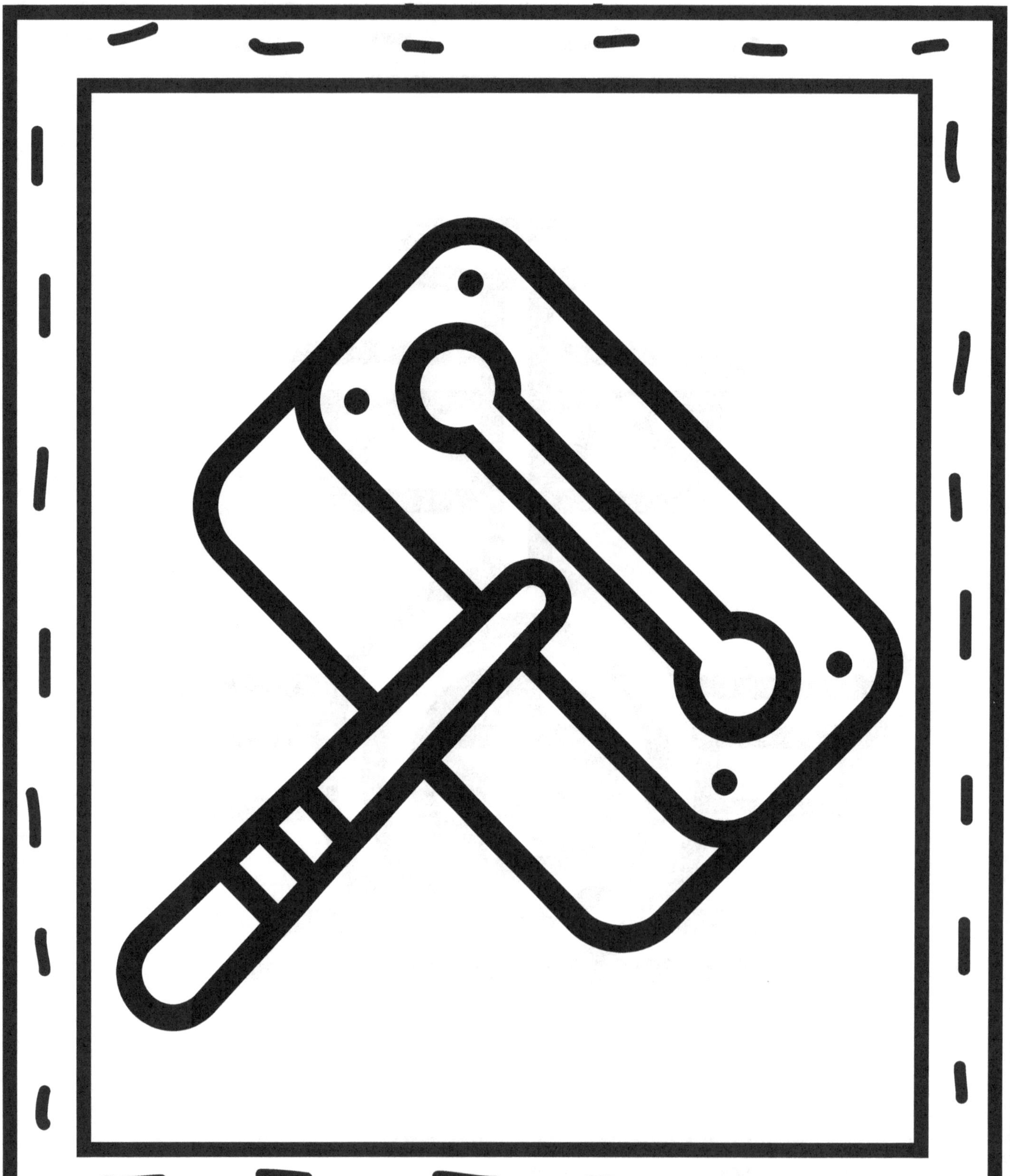

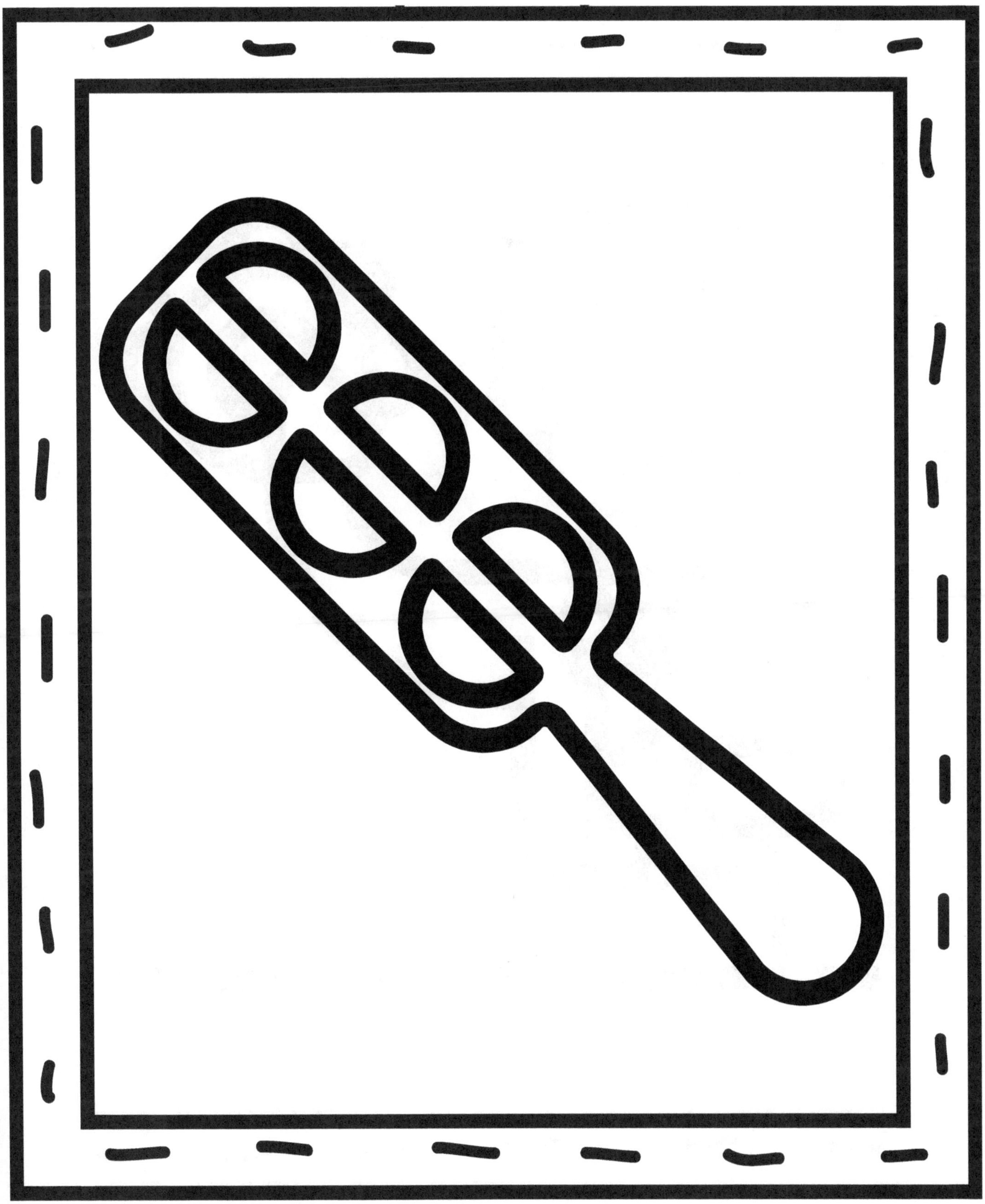

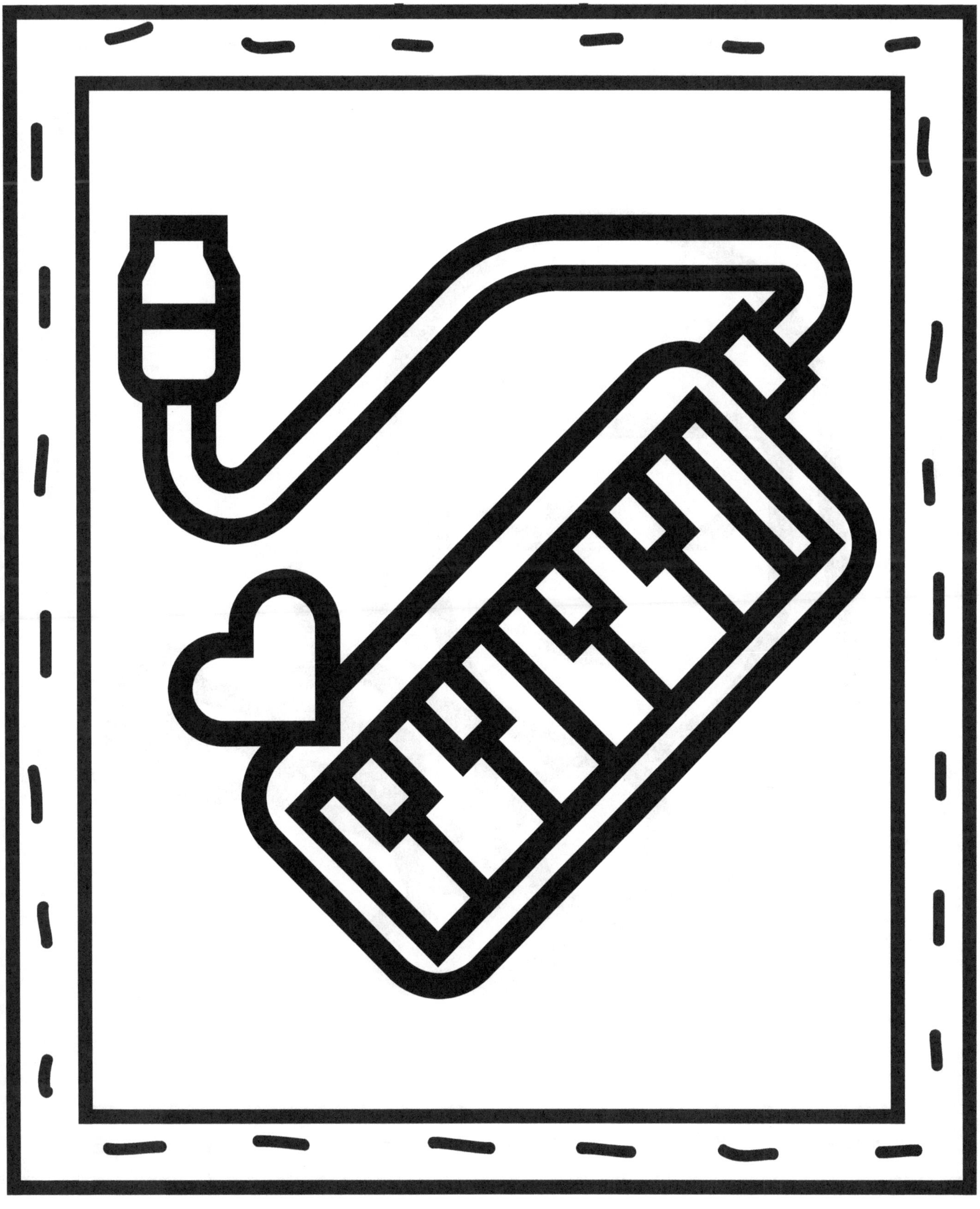

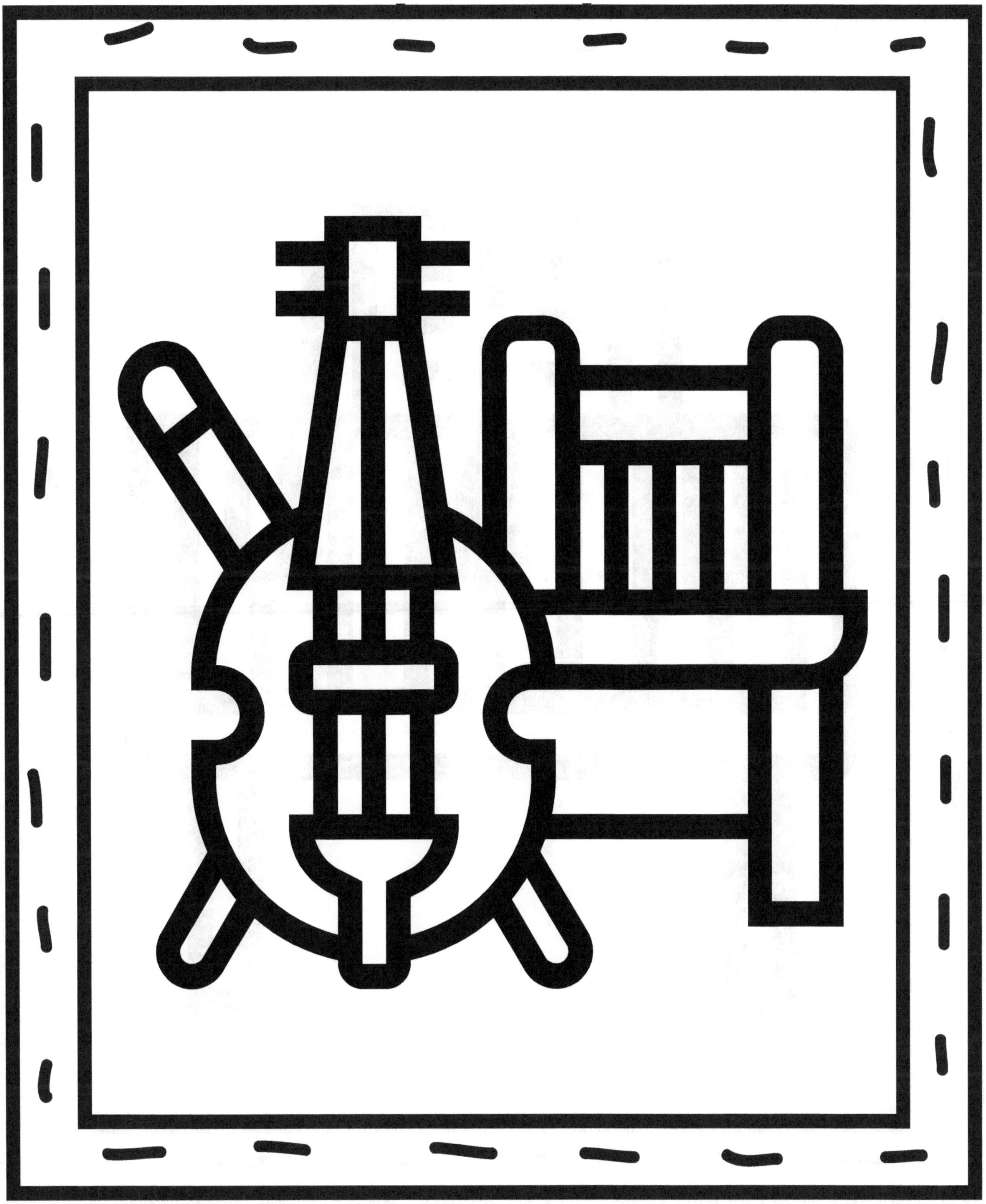

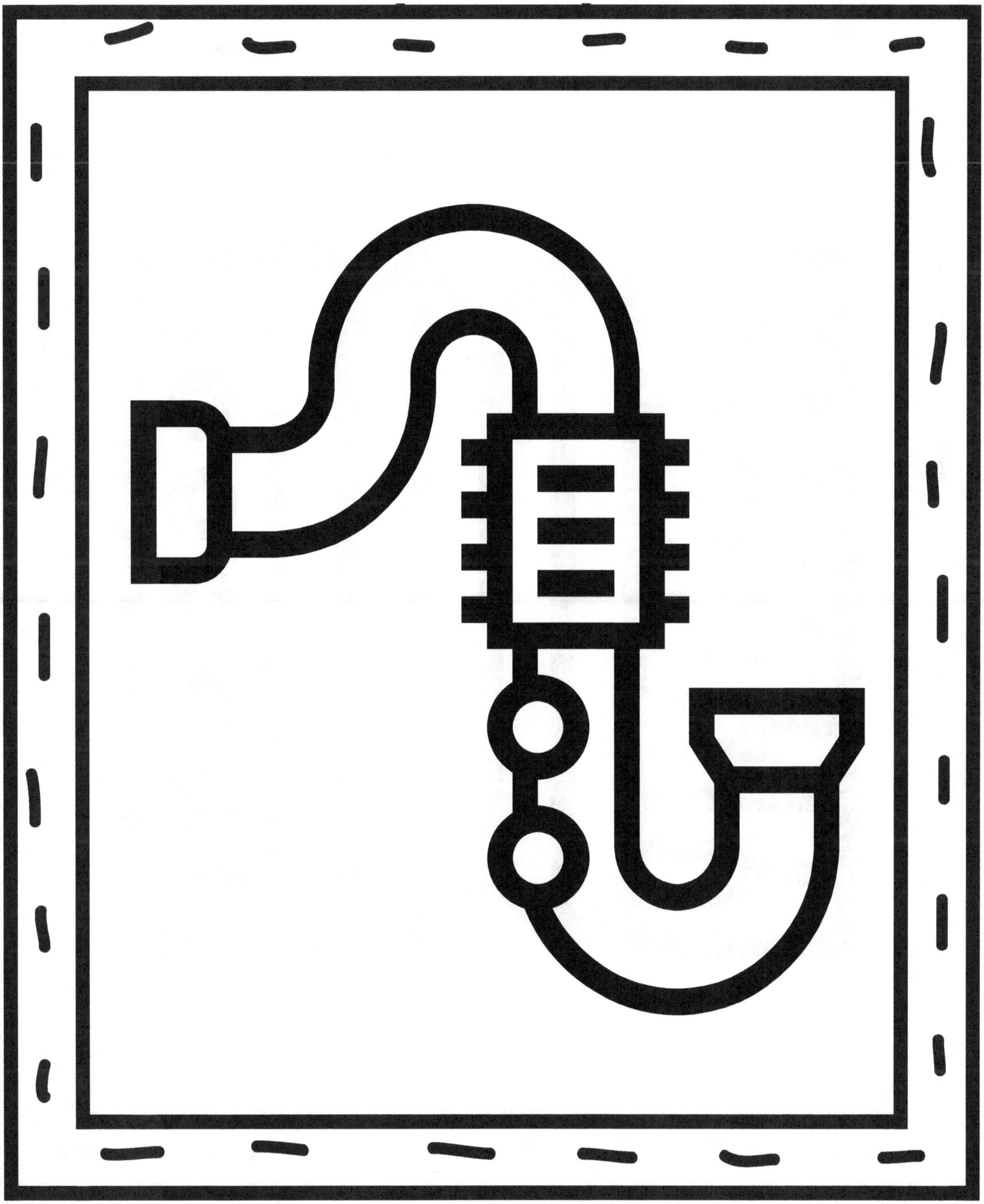

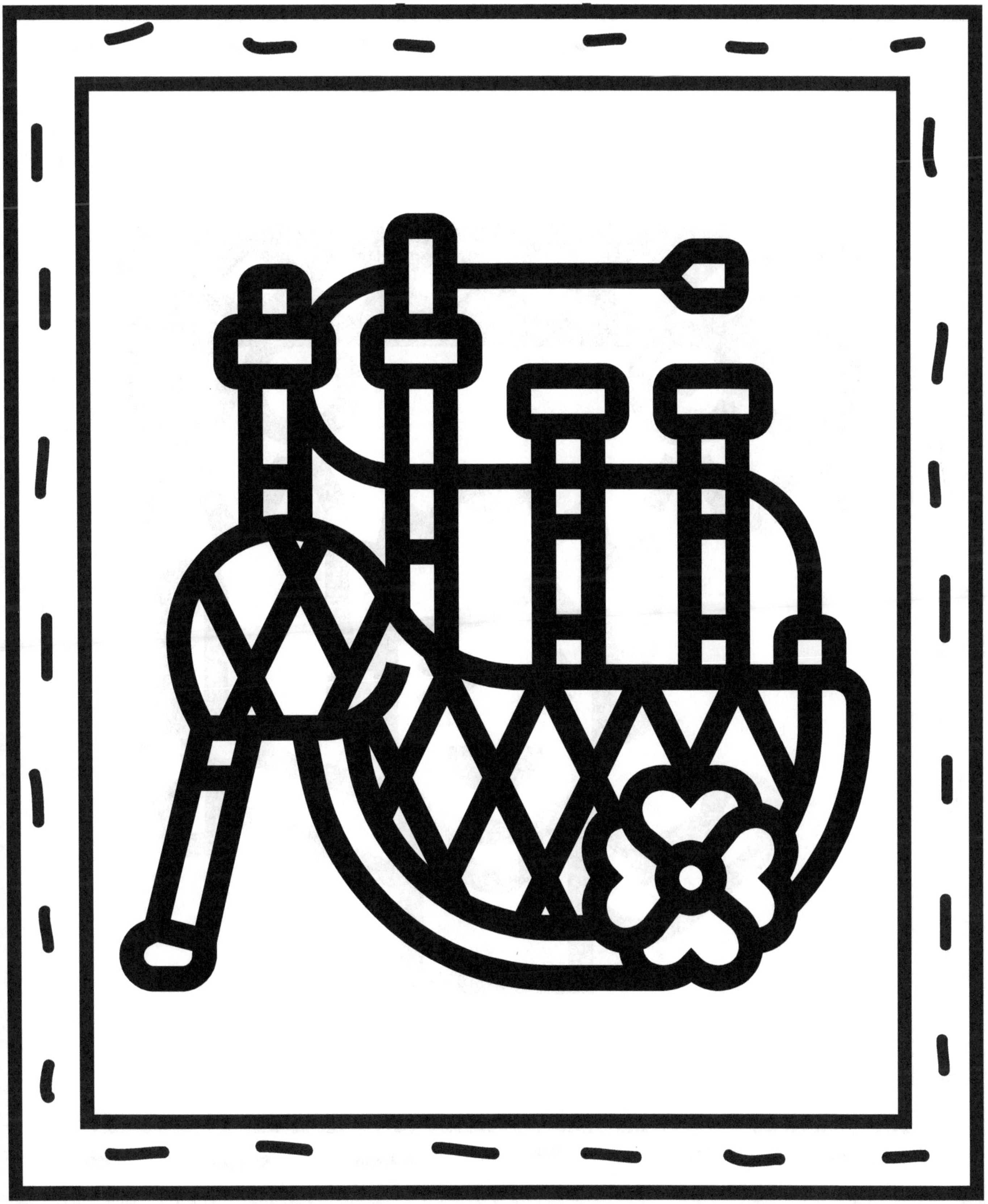

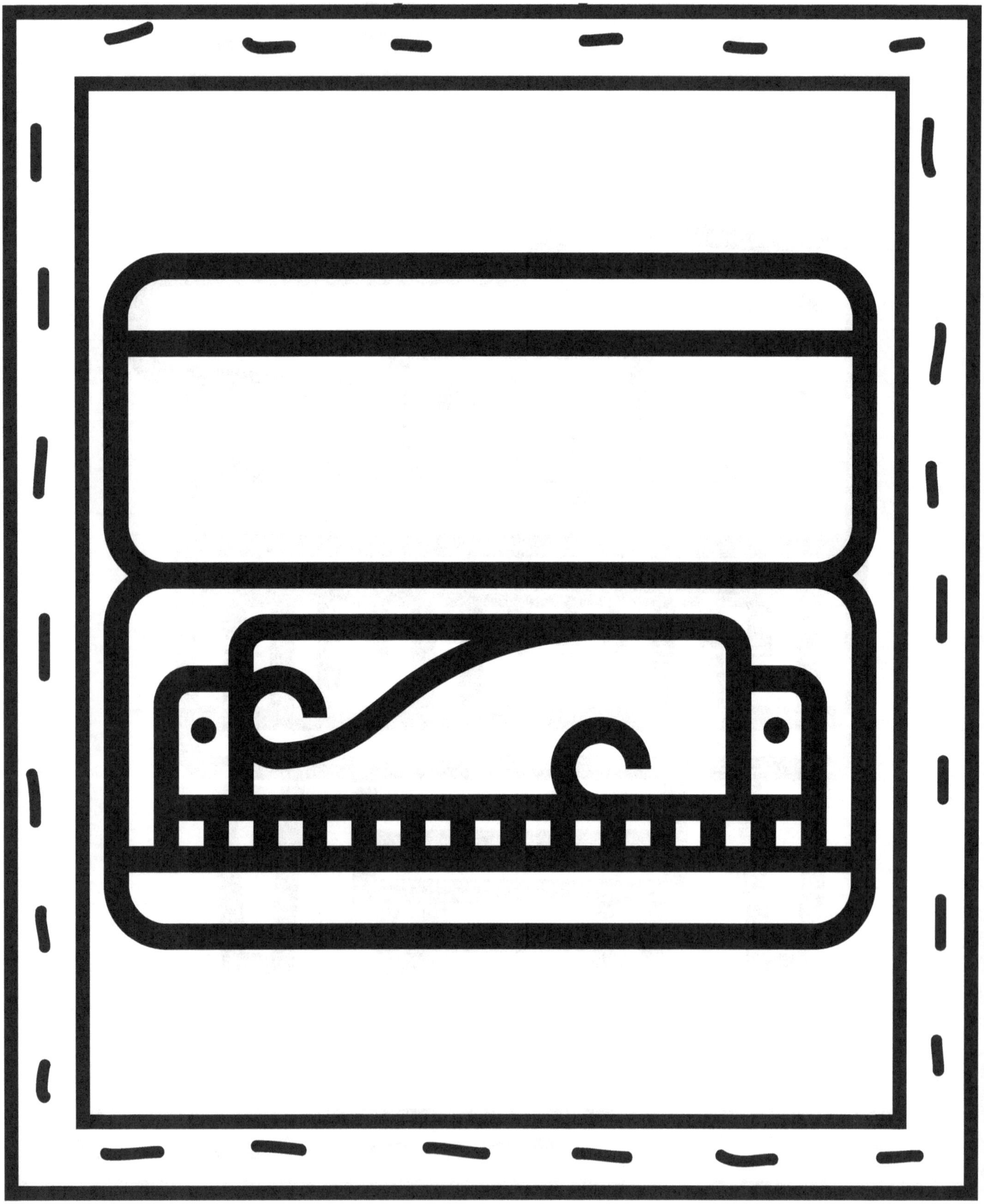

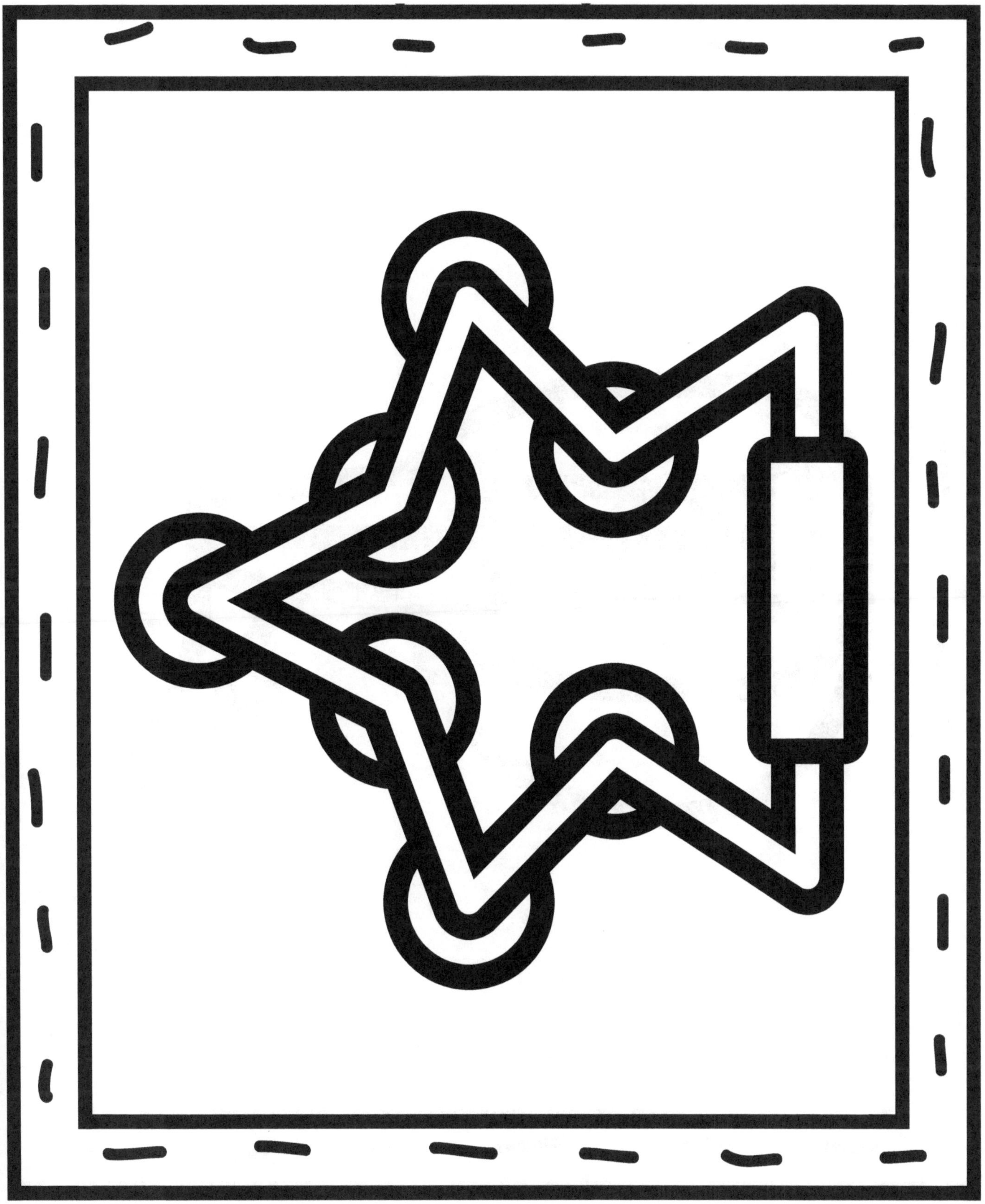

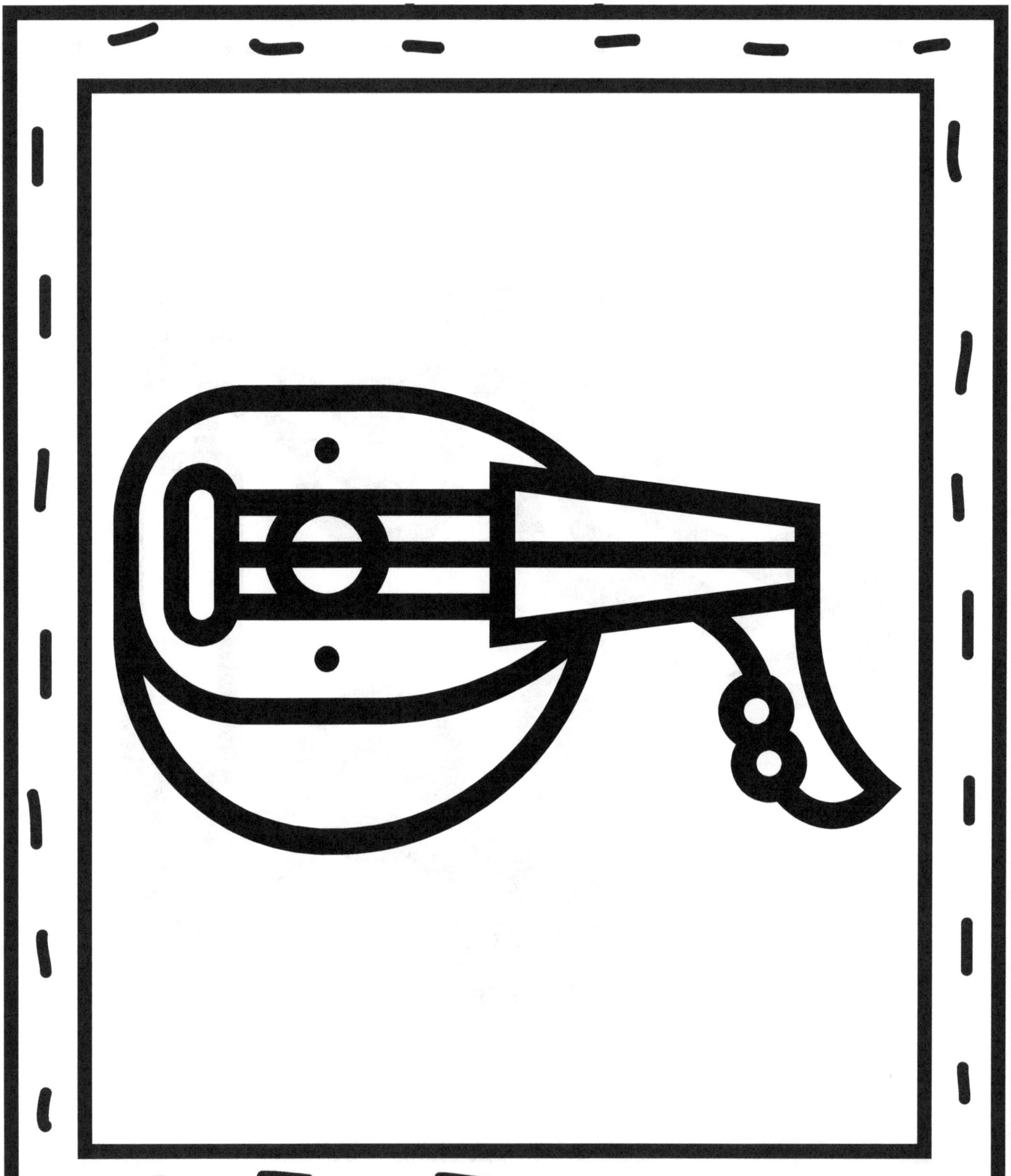

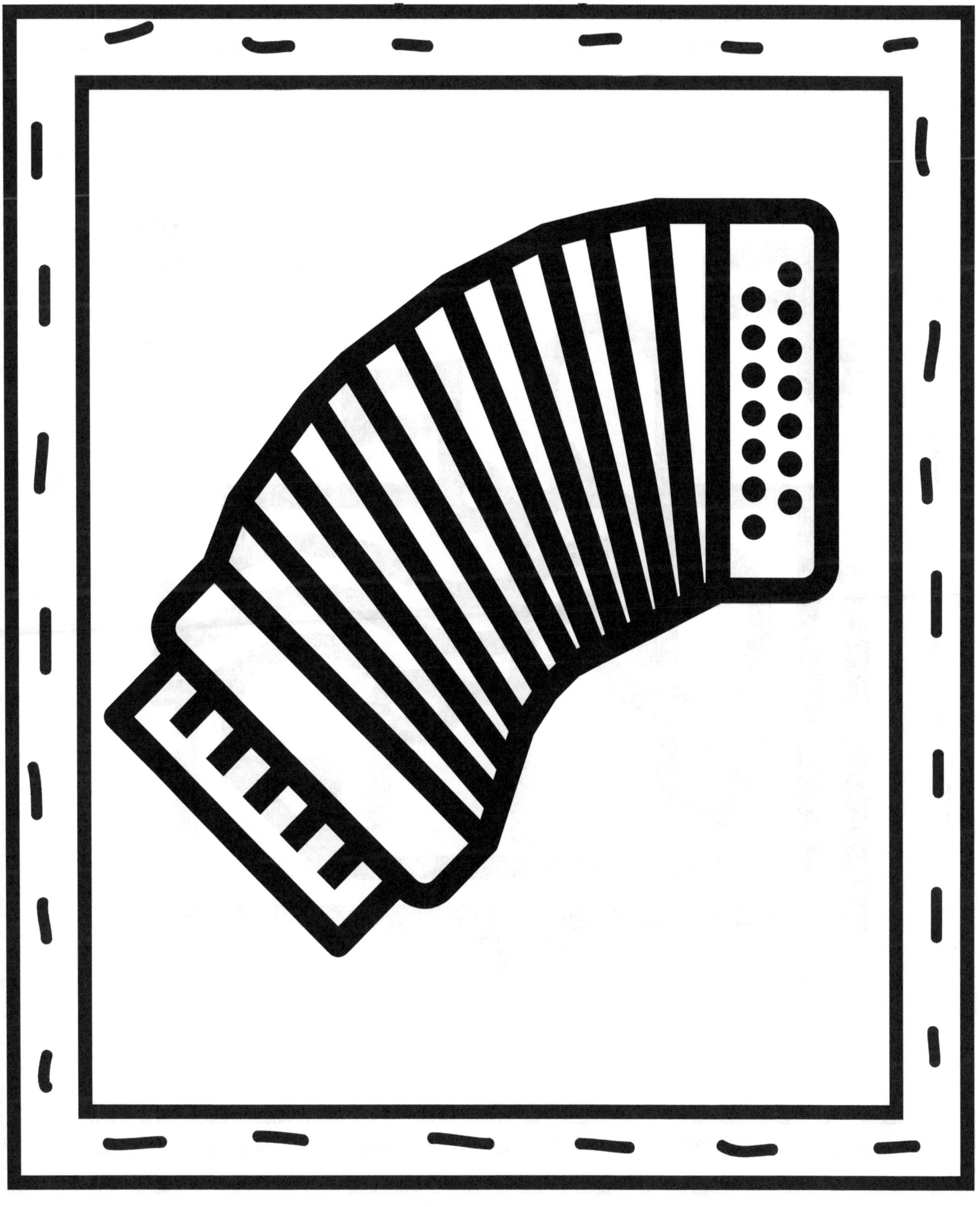

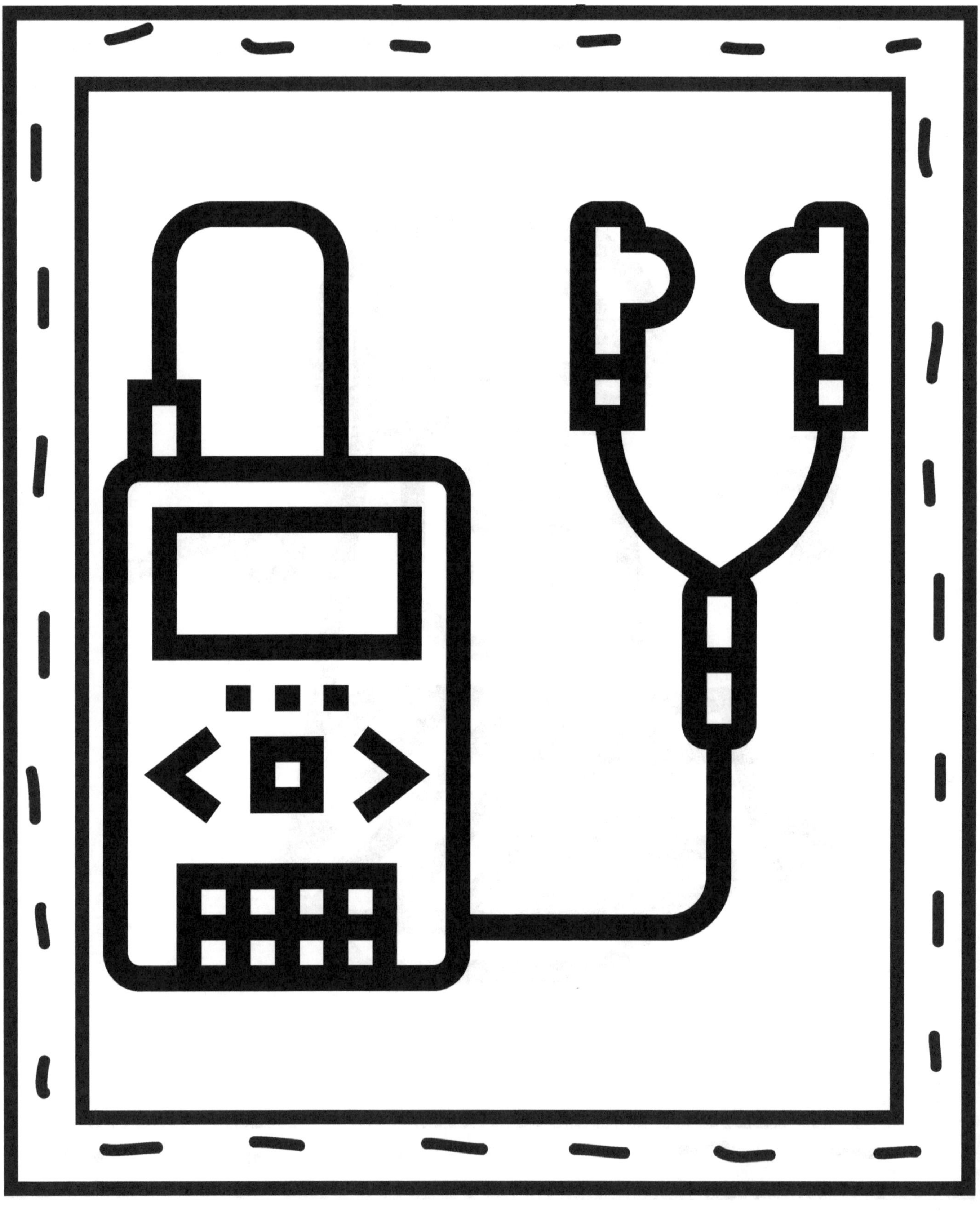

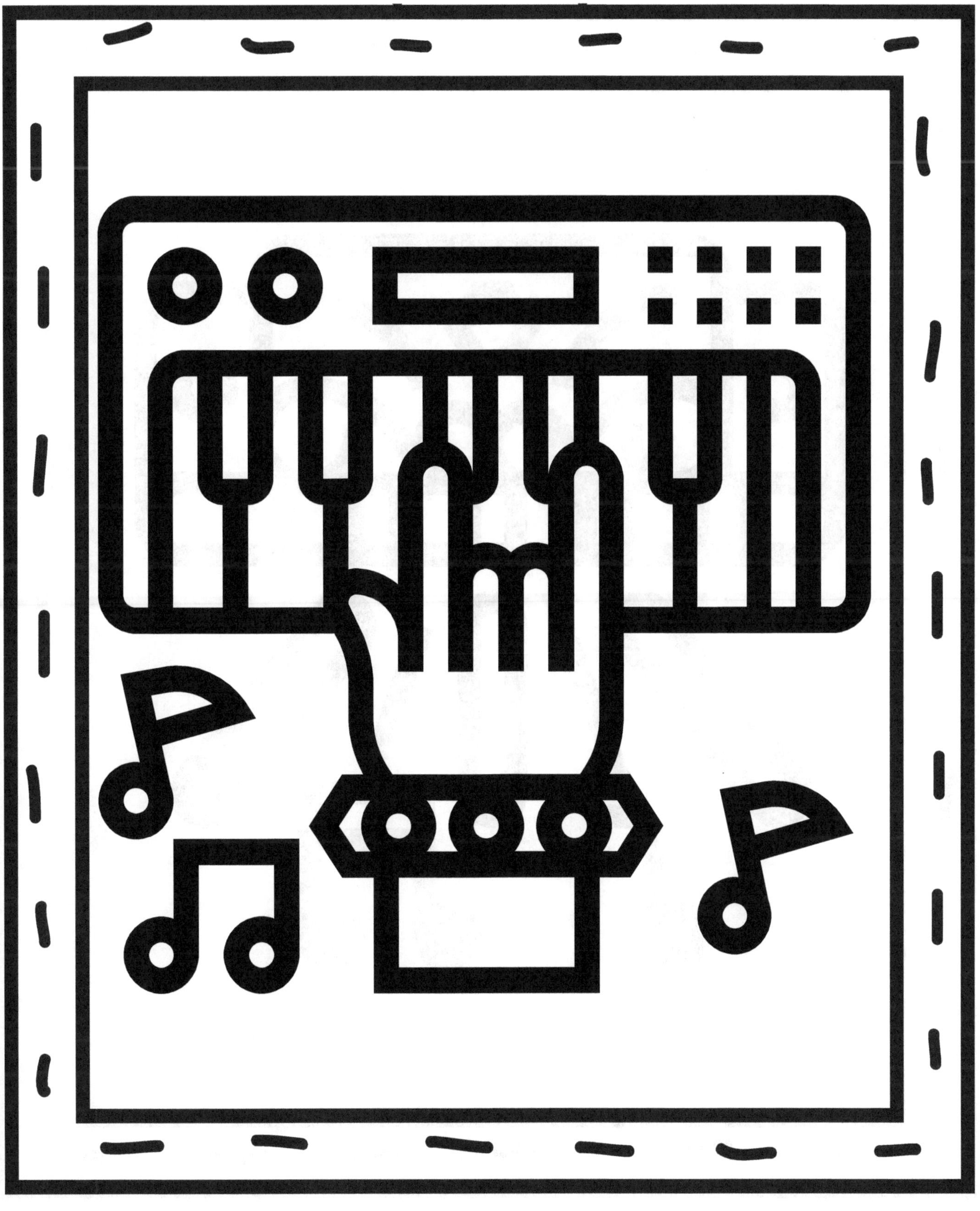

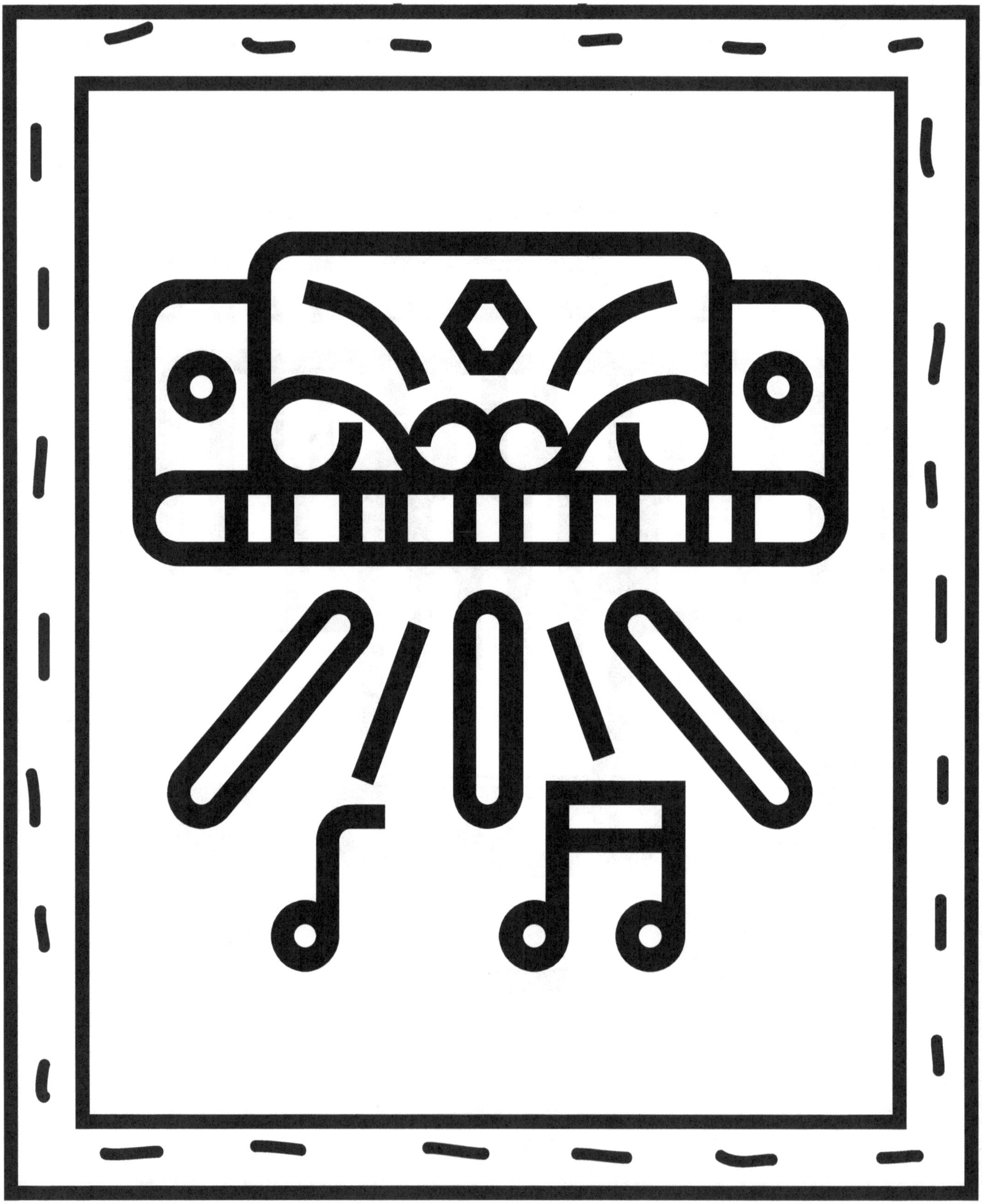

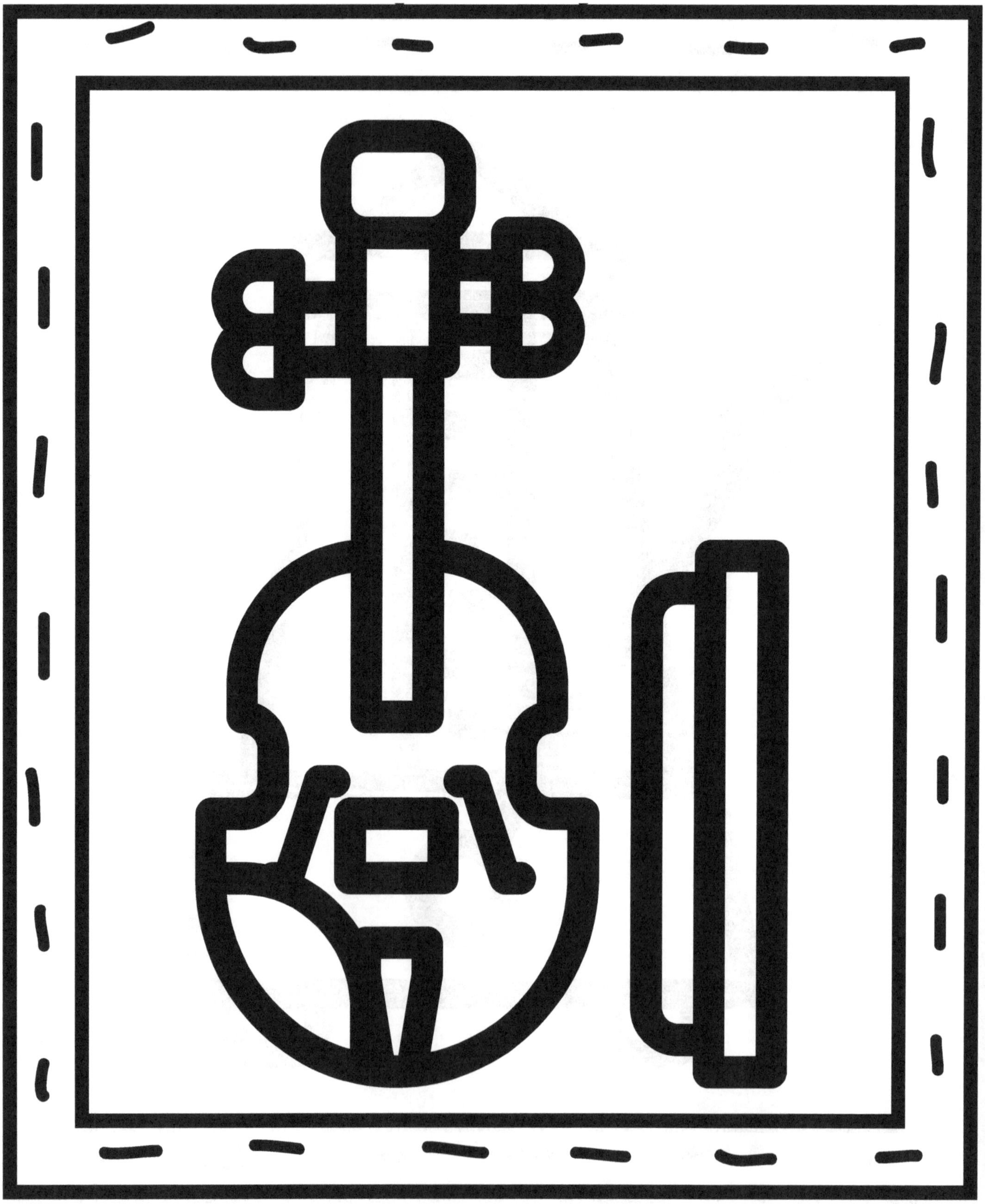

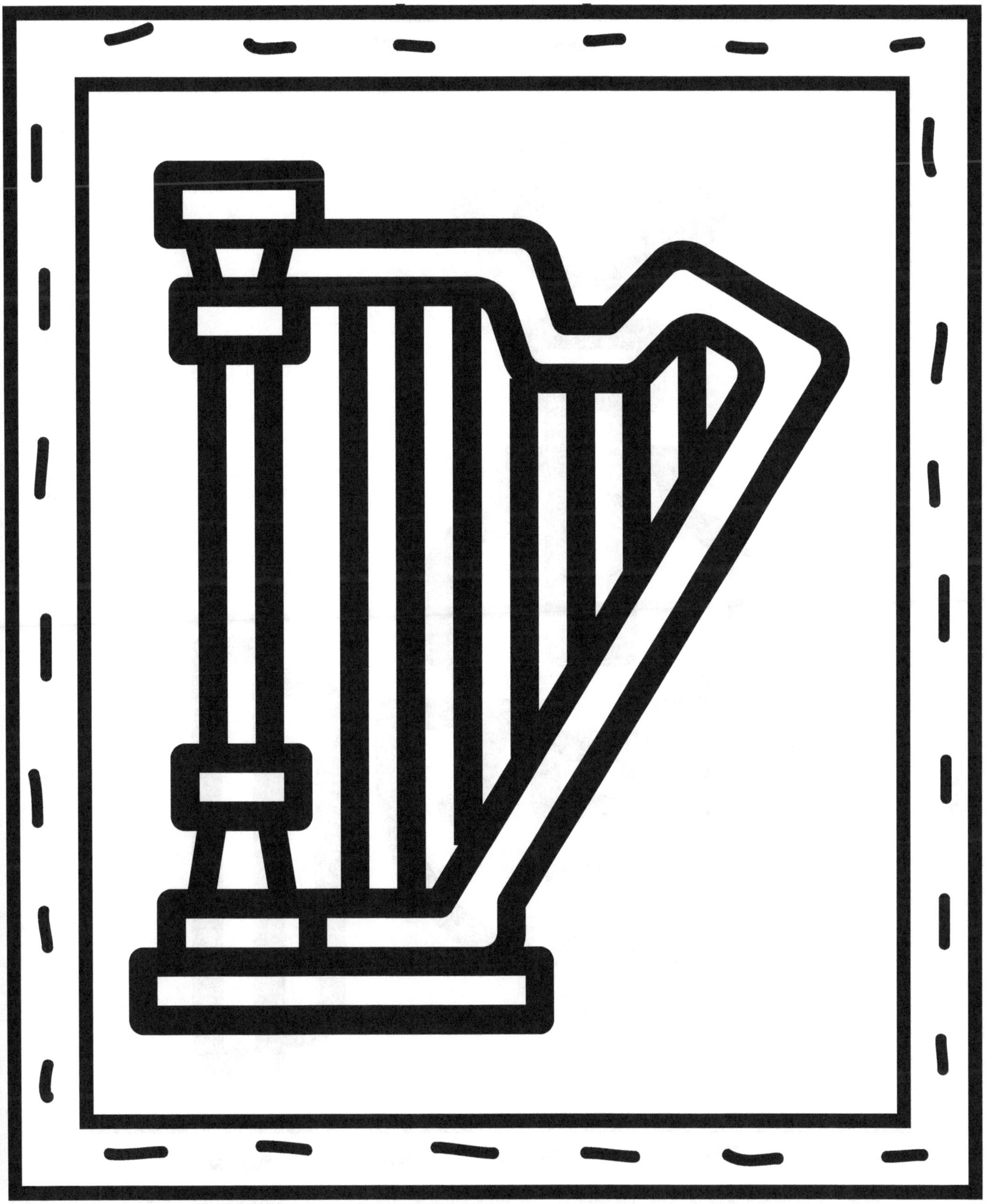

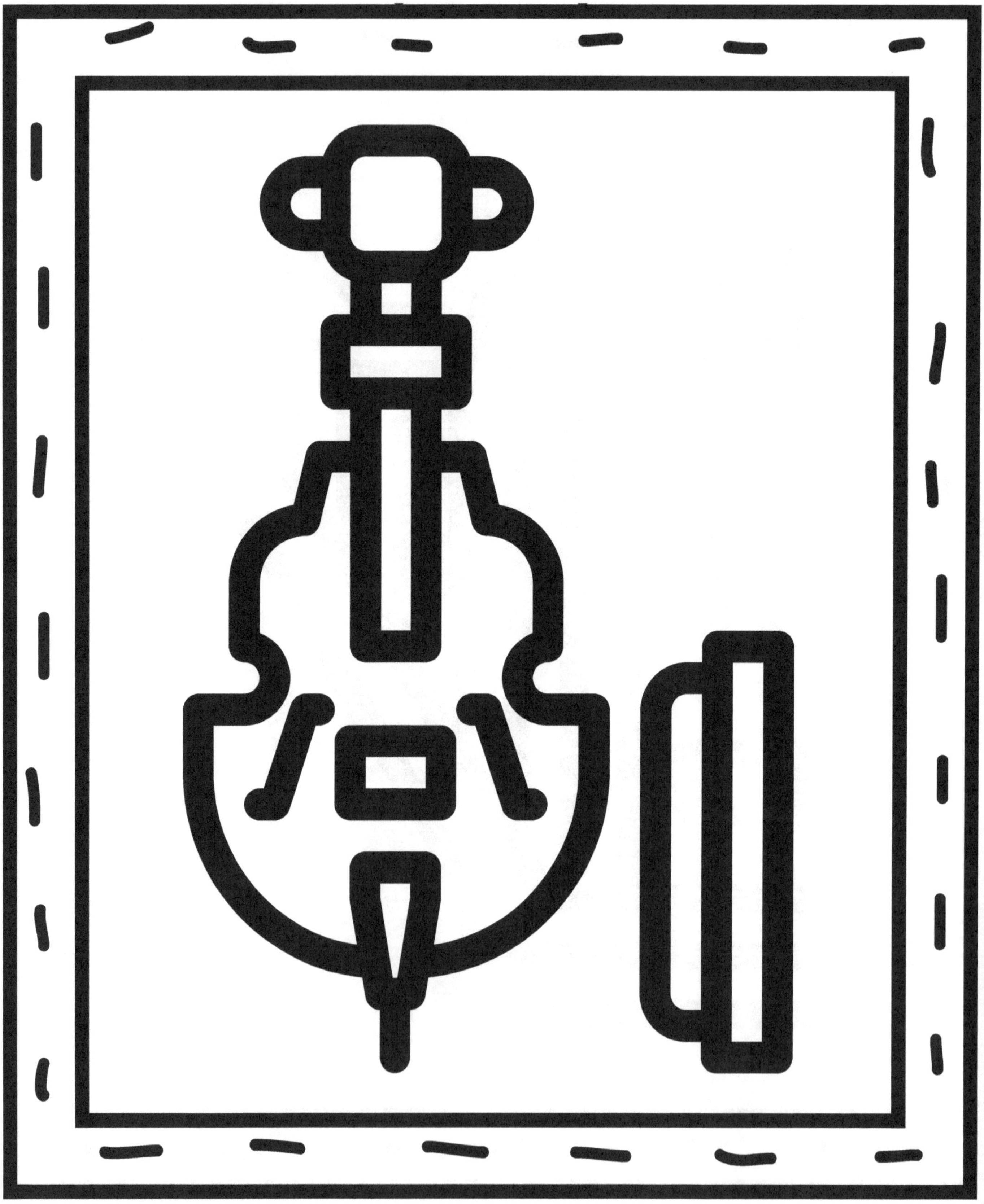

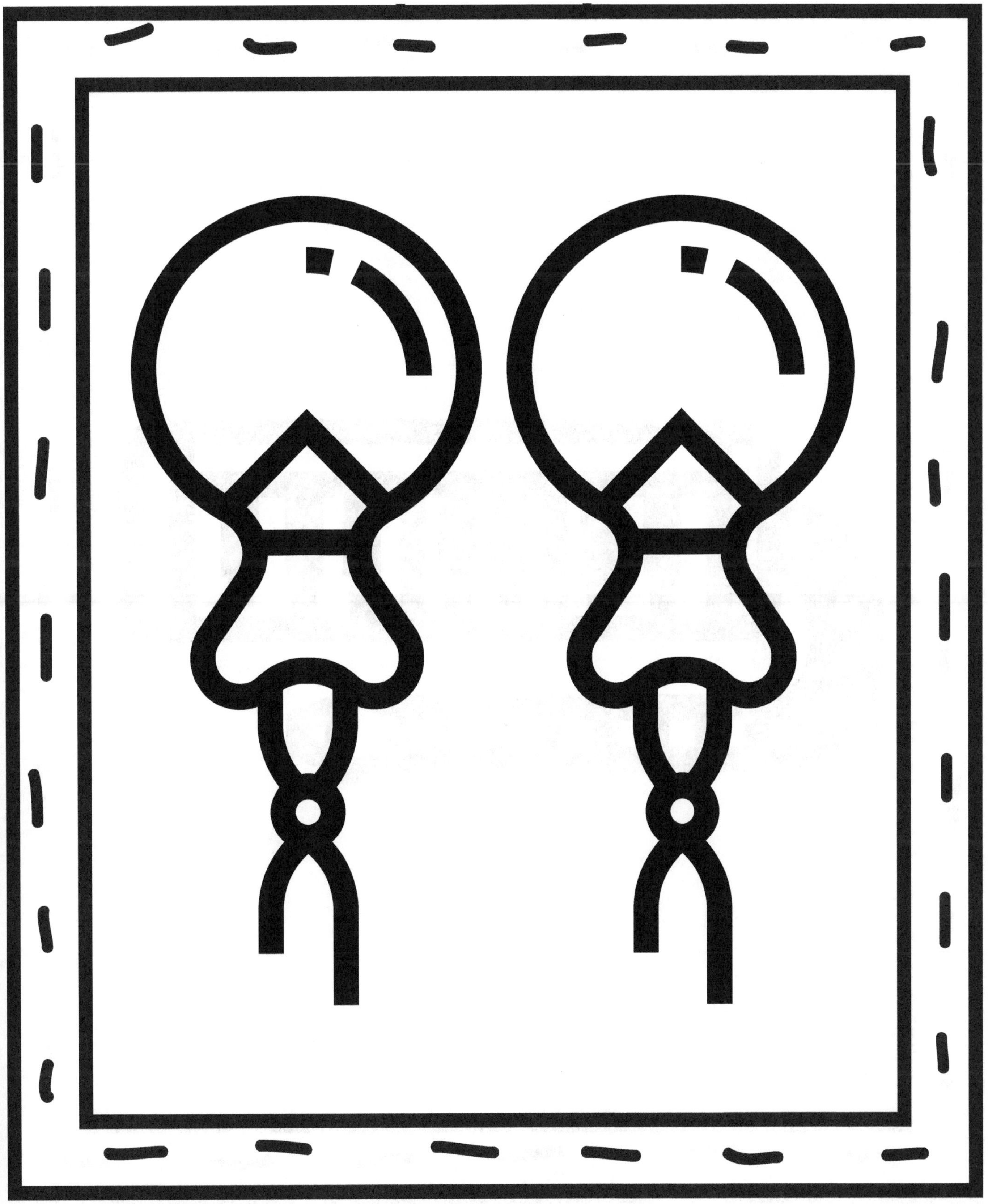

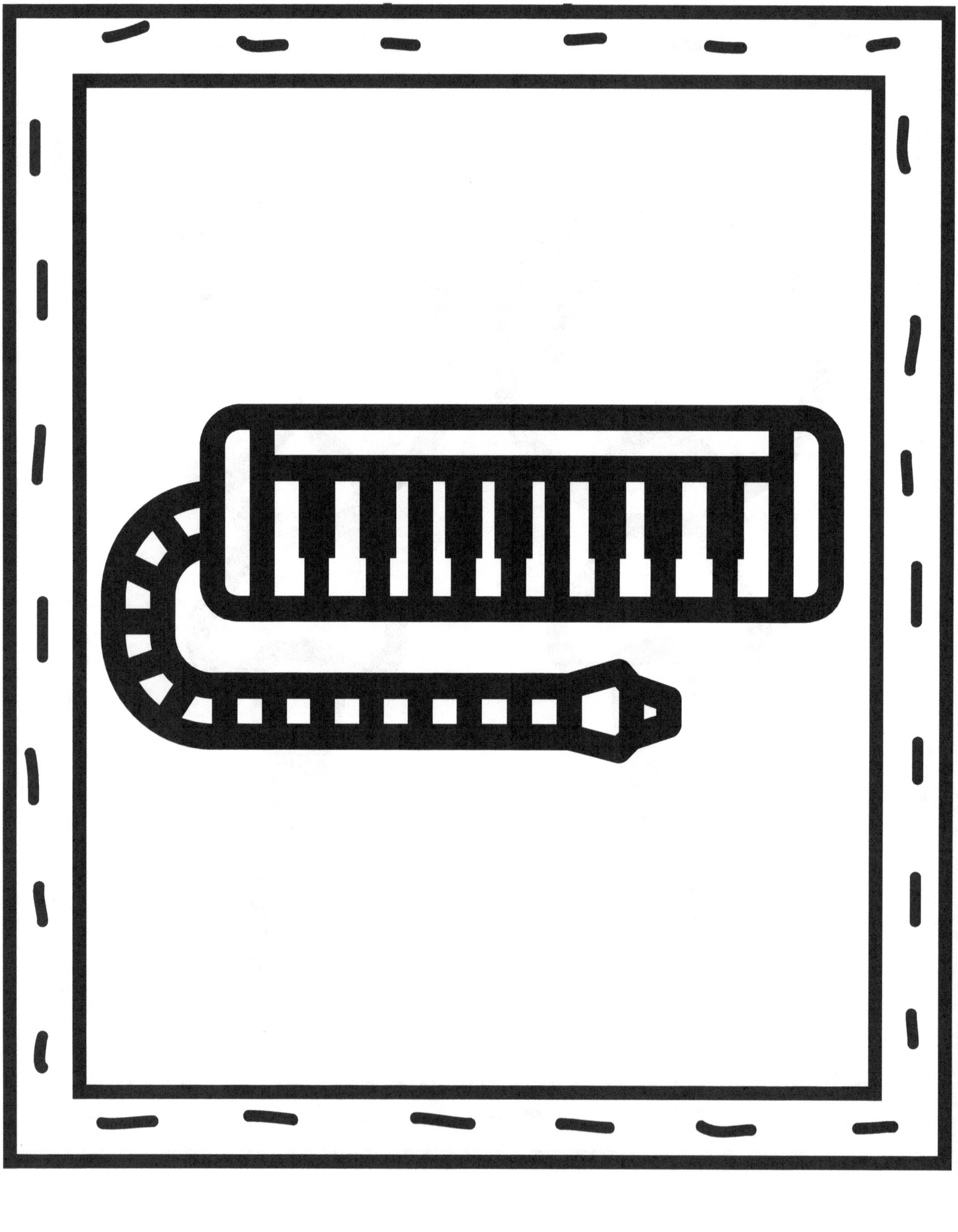

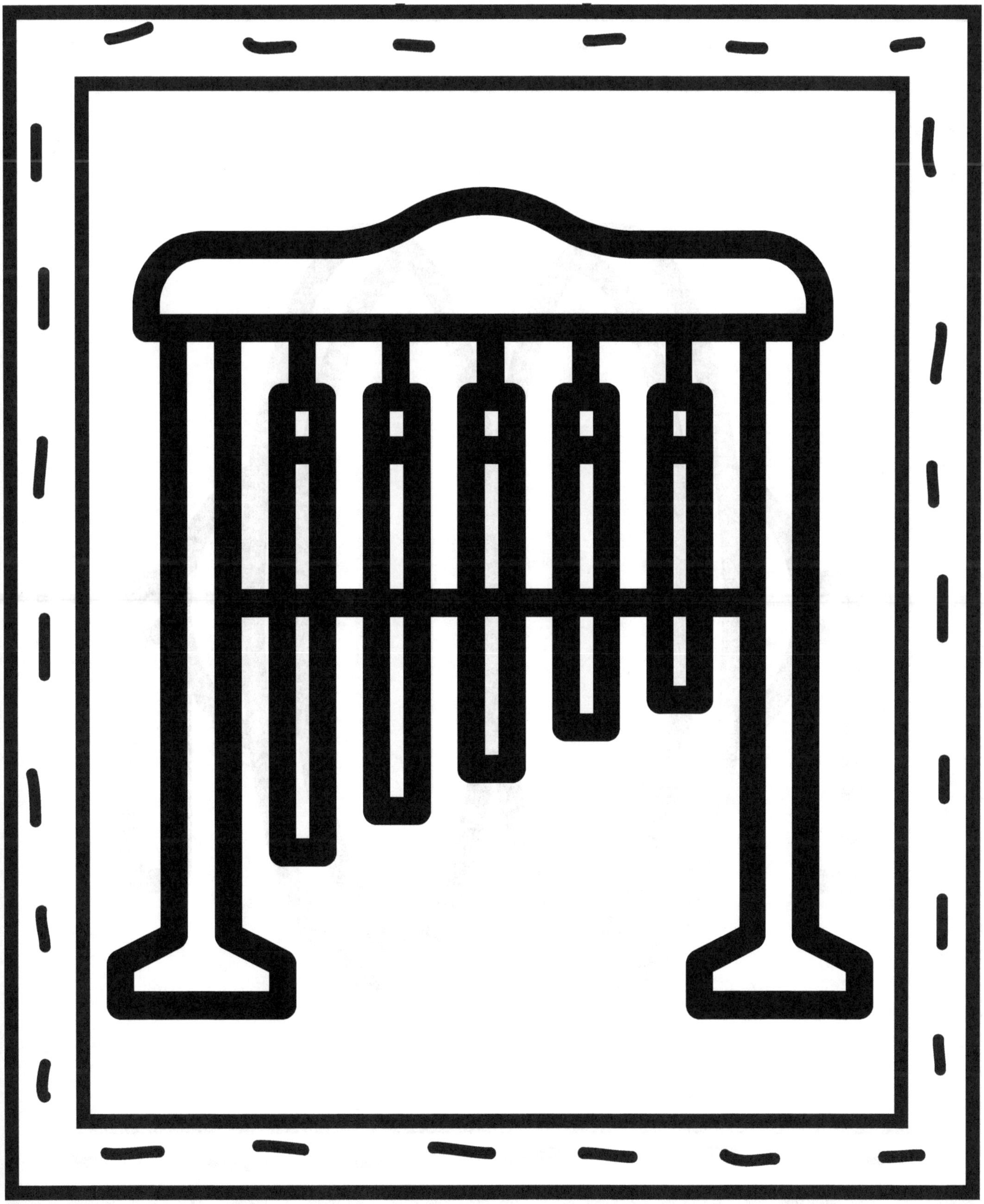

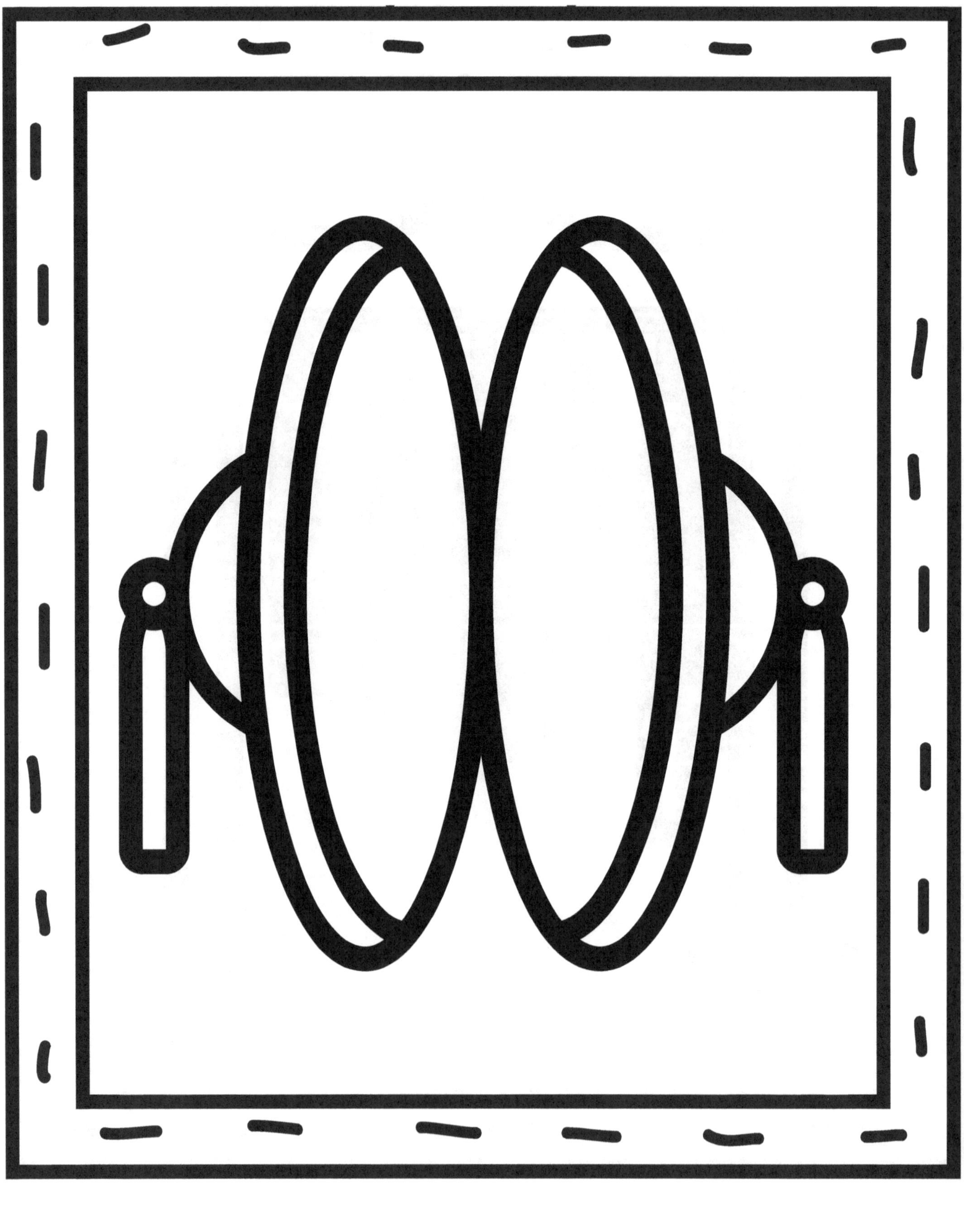

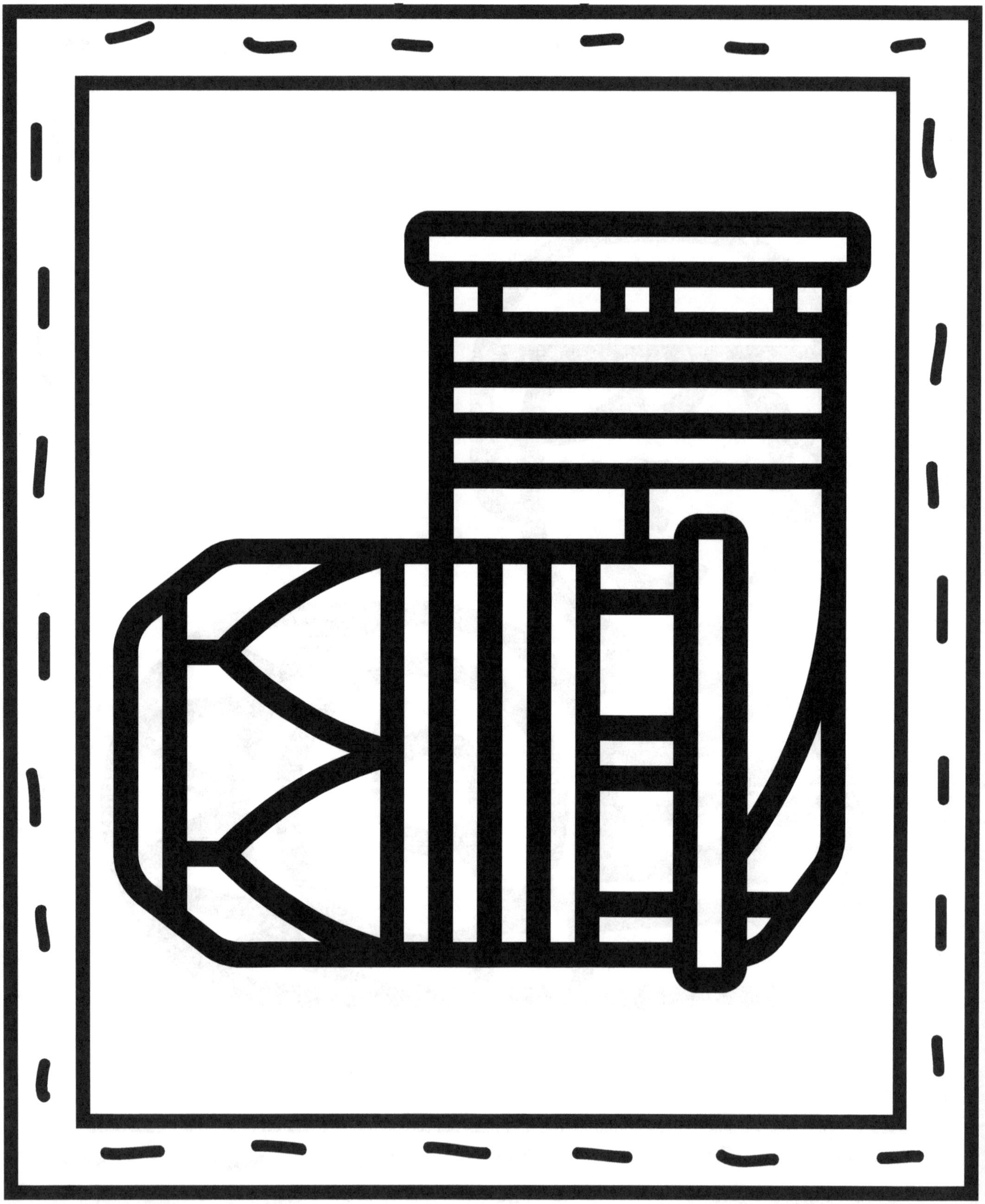

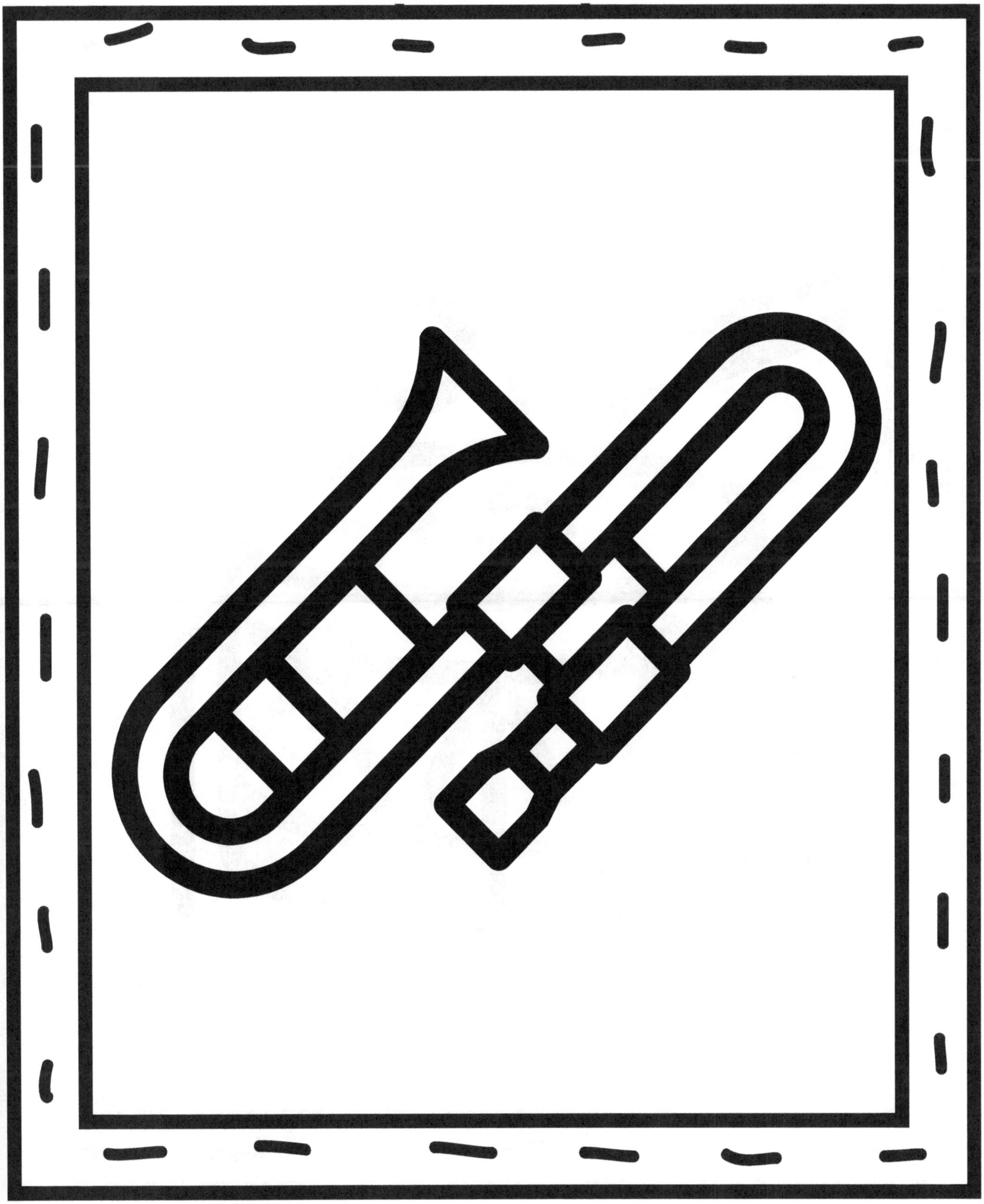

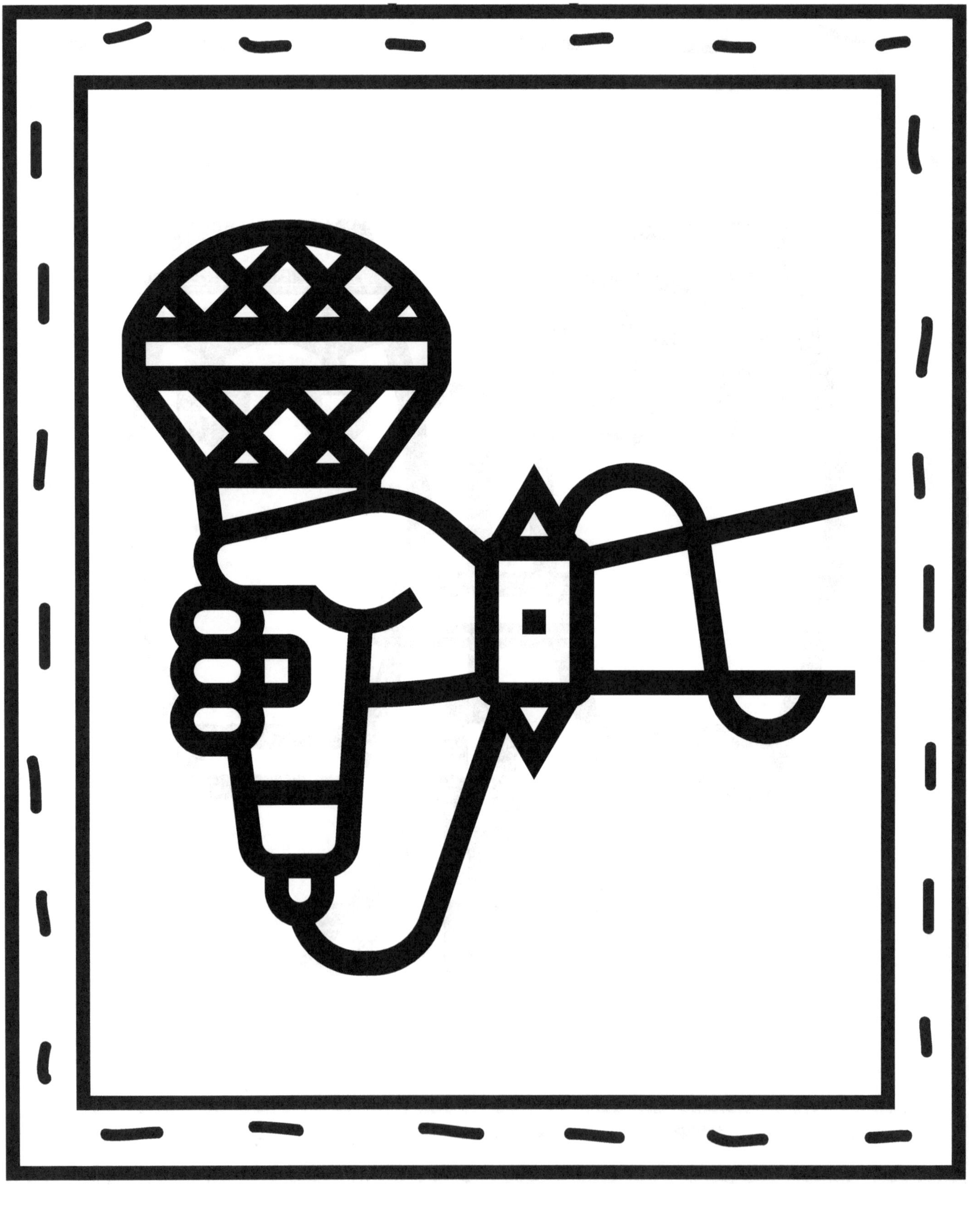

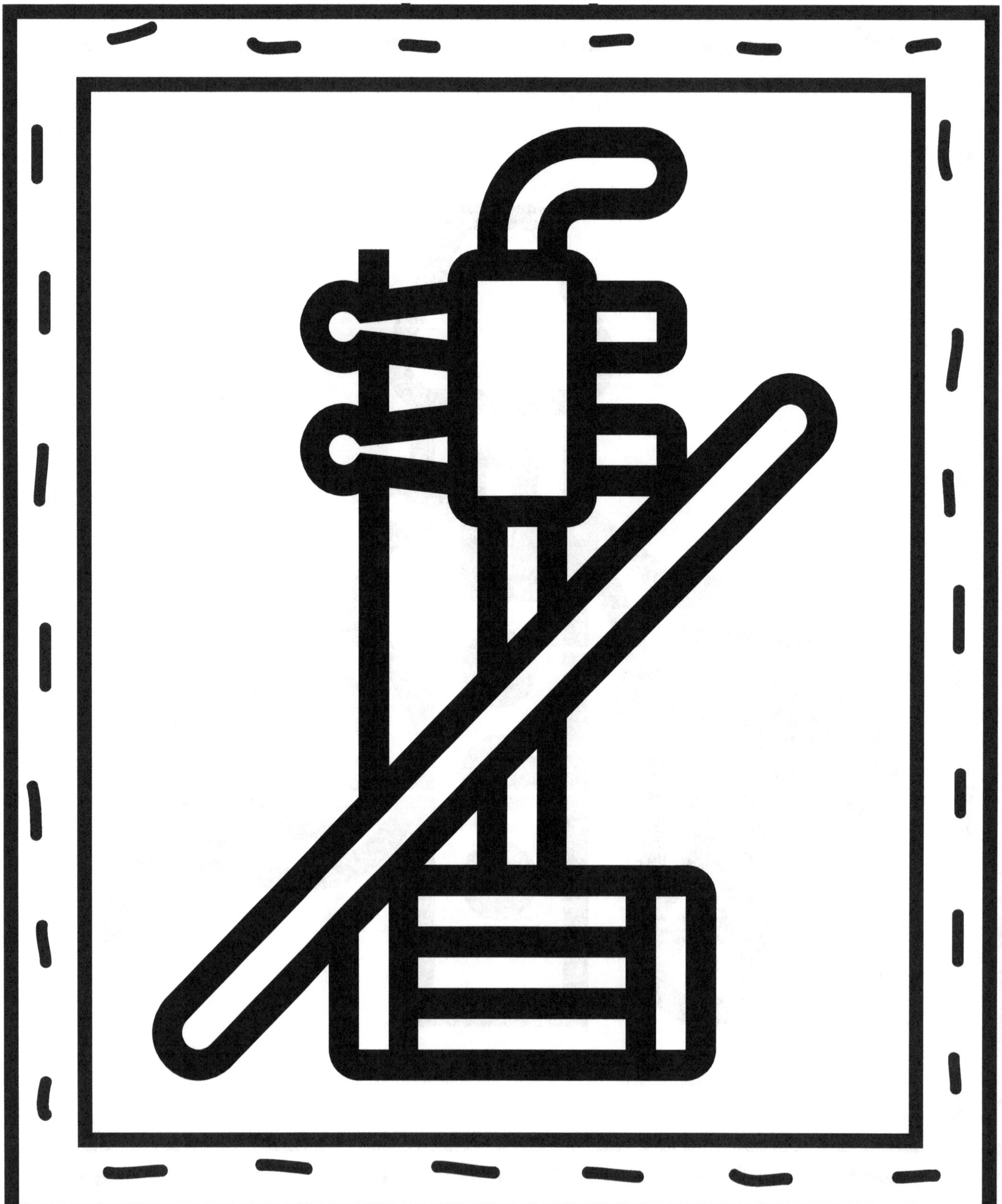

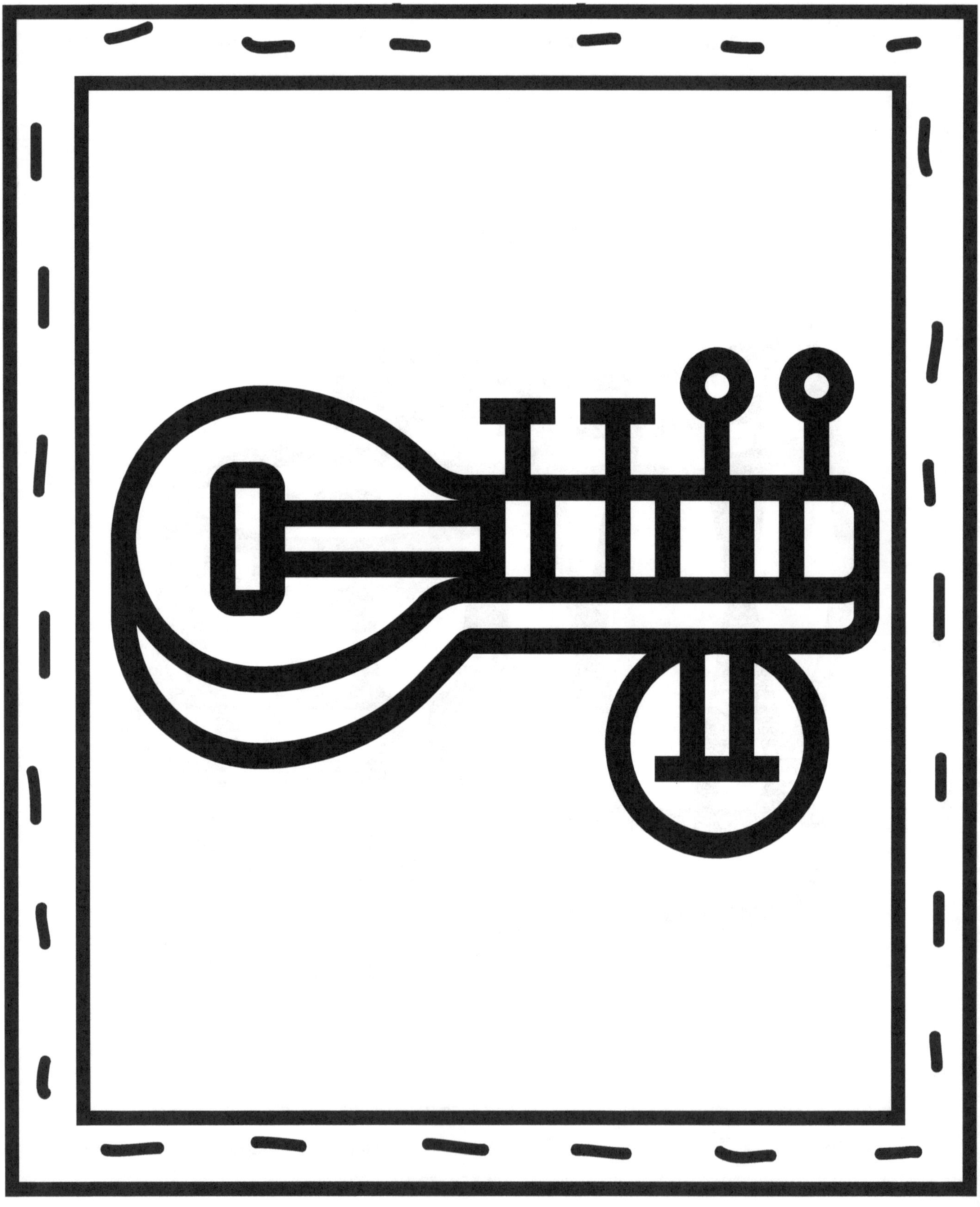

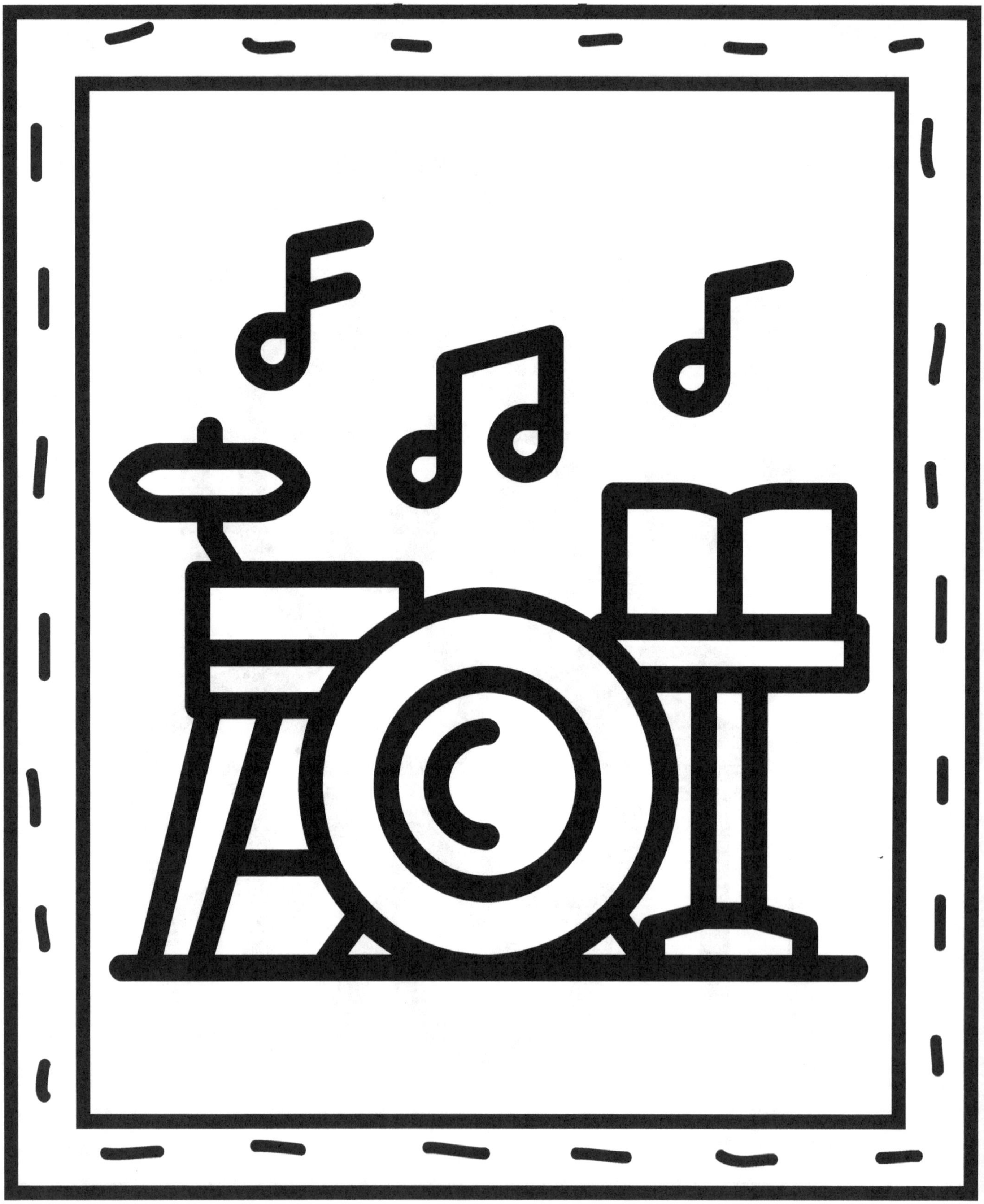

Made in United States
Troutdale, OR
11/02/2024

24374358R00058